This Faber book belongs to

....

....

For Pauline Ann, and for Emily, my first true reader — J.C

For Kyungchan and Momo — E.S

'When I got home tonight Emily was asking me to read it to her again . . . "Where's the Harry Hog book, Daddy?"'
Miles, and daughter Emily, age 3½

'I like, I really like it, 7 out of 10.' Enzo, age 5

'I love the cuttlefish cake.' Hector, age 5

'Reminded me of *Hairy Maclary* and *Zachary Quack*. Jacob loved it.'
Henry, and son Jacob, age 3 (almost)

'It's actually written by a poet, that's why the rhyming is so good.'
Santi, age 7, explaining it to his mum

'I love all the animals.' Jesse, age 3½

'My favourite is all the food!' Wilfie, age 3½

'It reminds me of *The Gruffalo*.' Sylvie, age 7

'I totally love the foggy bits, they're beautiful.'
Eva-May, age 5

'I liked it because it was about lots of animals and I like animals and I liked it because there was a party. I liked the pictures because they were beautiful. I liked the animals pulling the hog out of the mud.'
Sisters Maia, age 5 and Hannah, age 3

First published in the UK in 2014 by Faber and Faber Limited
Bloomsbury House, 74–77 Great Russell Street, London WC1B 3DA

Text copyright © Julia Copus, 2014
Illustration copyright © Eunyoung Seo, 2014

HB ISBN 978–0–571–31211–5
PB ISBN 978–0–571–30721–0

10 9 8 7 6 5 4 3 2

The moral rights of Julia Copus and Eunyoung Seo have been asserted.
A CIP record for this book is available from the British Library.

→ A FABER PICTURE BOOK ←

A
Harry
& Lil
Story

Hog in the Fog

Julia Copus

Illustrated by
Eunyoung Seo

ff

FABER & FABER

This is the story of Candy Stripe Lil
and Harry the Hog who lived over the hill

to
HARR
THE
HOG

. . . and a foggy March day, round about three,
when Lil had invited Harry for tea.

Lil had been busy for hours and hours
piling the treats up in teetering towers.

And now, all of Harry's favourite snacks
were heaped on the table in wobbling stacks.

There was southern-fried lizard
and earwig fudge,
a very large bowl of barnacle sludge;

there were chocolate-chip beetles and slug-flavoured chips
and warm jellied maggots with fruit-flavoured dips;
dragonflies' tongues and a frothy muck-shake
and leeches on sticks and a cuttlefish cake.

Well, three o'clock came . . .

  then a quarter past three,

but still Harry hadn't turned up for his tea.

Outside the window, for miles around,
a ghostly haze hung over the ground.
"Oh dear!" cried Lil. "Even Harry the Hog
could get himself lost in the thick of that fog."

When Harry still hadn't arrived by four
poor Lil didn't think she could wait any more.
So she pulled down her candy-striped cap from its hook,
put on her raincoat and set off to look.

Pittery pattery,
tippety tappety,
off up the hill
went Candy Stripe Lil.

A sheep sauntered by with her nose to the ground,
munching the grass with a soft crunch sound.
"Excuse me," said Lil, stepping out of her way,
"Have you seen a hog on your travels today?"

"I have not," said the sheep. "But a while back I saw
what I *think* was a hedge, where no hedge was before.
A hog in the fog won't be easy to find.
Why don't I help? I can look out behind."

So pittery pattery,
tippety tappety,
munch crunch,
munch crunch,
on up the hill
went the sheep and Lil.

A deer came stepping into the lane.
Tac tac went his hooves, like the tapping of rain.
"Can I ask," said Lil to the deer, "if I may:
have *you* seen a hog on your travels today?"

"All I saw," said the deer, "were the wings of a bat.
Or I *think* they were wings. They were pinkish and flat.
You'll need all the help you can get in this weather.
If I come along, we can all look together."

So pittery pattery,
tippety tappety,
munch crunch,
tac tac tac,
on up the hill
went the three of them till . . .

A blue-black crow swooped
over the ground
and perched on a tree,
with a loud qwark sound.

"Can I ask," Lil called to the crow, "if I may:
have *you* seen a hog on your travels today?"
"Not a hog," squawked the crow. "All I saw was a snake
fast asleep on a log – what I *think* was a snake.

"We crows have a wonderful view from the sky.
Would you like me to help? I can look while I fly."

Crow stretched out his wings,
took off from his perch
and circled around
to join in the search.

Pittery pattery,
tippety tappety,
munch crunch,
tac tac tac,
qwaa–aark . . .

through the gathering dark,
through the gloopy, soupy thick of the fog,
all four went searching for Harry the Hog.

By now it was colder; Lil let out a . . . sneeze!
A wind was astir in the tops of the trees.
As they felt their way forward
and tried to go quicker,

the fog got thicker . . .

and thicker . . .

and . . .

thicker.

Pittery pattery,
tippety —

Stop!

Around the next corner,
cocooned in the fog, was a . . .
THING of some kind,
half sunk in a bog.

"It's the bush!" cried Sheep.
"It's the bat!" cried Deer.
"It's the snake!" squawked Crow. "It's quite plain from up here."

"Whatever it is," cried Lil, "it's STUCK!"
And they all started hauling it out of the muck,
shoving and heaving to lift the THING clear,

Lil at the front

and Sheep at the rear.

Inch by inch, bog-soaked, mud-smeared,
more and more of the creature appeared.

Until, with a nudge,
with a pull and a push,

one half of the THING
emerged with a whoosh!

Then slippily, slurpily,
gluggily, gurgly,
out of the bog came . . .

Harry the Hog!

He told them his story – how he'd walked through the fog
and gone snout-over-trotters into the bog.

"So you see," he went on, "after all of that tumbling,
it's hardly surprising my tummy is rumbling.
I thank you most kindly for rescuing me.

"Now, I wonder . . ." he said,
"Is there still time for tea?"

. . . And there was.

"Here at my house," said Lil with a smile,
"it stays TEA o'clock for a *very* long while.
There's more than enough to go round, as you see.
Let the party begin! We can ALL have tea!"